Why is No One Following Me?

Techniques taught by
executive leadership coaches
to muscle-up your leadership

James Johnson
Matt Rush
Angela Johnson

Ketch Publishing
Bloomington, IN

ISBN: 978-0-9801420-3-7

Ketch Publishing

4675 N. Benton Dr.
Bloomington, Indiana

www.KetchPublishing.com

Dedicated to our Grandparents

Lessons in leadership are best learned

from las Abuelas y los Abuelos.

A special thanks to
Editor Jim Bullock, PhD.

Table of Contents

 # Introduction

Henry Ford said, "No one built a reputation based upon what they were going to do." We say, "Well said Mr. Ford!" If you walk into any bookstore, the one thing that you are assured to find is row after row of books on leadership, there are literally THOUSANDS!

So why do you need one more?

For starters, look behind you. How many people are following you? Maybe we should ask, are there as many people following you as there should be? Very rarely is our rear view mirror operating at full capacity.

Secondly, this is **not** another book on leadership. You already know the theories and principles. In fact, if you are like most people who aspire to be better leaders, you have stacks of books on the subject. What you need are the applications, the nuts and bolts, the 'How To's. This is a training manual, use it as such. Within the cover of this book, you are going to find a series of exercises that will give you the opportunity to put your leadership into action. Some exercises are quite simple, others will require a degree of sacrifice, and all will have a dramatic and drastic impact on your leadership and the number of people you are leading.

For the past 10 years, we at The Ethos Leadership Group have been growing and refining these exercises. This book is not an aspirin that will simply make you feel better for a little while and then let you slip right back to where you were. If you will take these exercises one at a time, put the principles into use, and fill out the action plan at the end of each chapter, you will change your life. After you have worked on yourself, use these exercises to facilitate others or do them together with your core group of friends. Then, log on to our website (www.ethosleadership.com) and let us know how you did.

It does not matter how many leadership books you read or seminars you attend, they will not **change** you unless **you** put the applications to work in your everyday leadership practice.

Don't forget, **you** are responsible for your leadership, get out there and **build** that reputation!

Why is no one following you?

# Chapter 1

Identifying the Attributes
of Your Best Leadership

Commit to getting better everyday.

Jim Leek

The Personal Foundation
for Your Most Powerful Leadership

The strongest part of any home is always the foundation. No matter what storms wreck havoc above ground, the foundation remains strong, stable, and unmovable. As leaders, we are no different. This exercise helps identify the unique attributes within you that will produce your strongest leadership. Making a practice of following this exercise helps vital keys of leadership, including self-discipline, self-accountability, reflection, modeling, and daily action steps. This is the most requested exercise from our clients who want to enhance their personal leadership and unlock new dimensions of personal effectiveness.

Your 6 Attributes of Leadership

1. Make a list (4-6 names) of the people who have had the greatest influence on your life.

2. Beside each name, write the first attribute that comes to mind when you think about that person. Examples might include generosity, peacemaker, volunteerism, etc.

3. Re-write the list of attributes on an index card or place it in your PDA.

4. Read the list three times a day, every day (yes, even Saturday and Sunday.)

Person	**Attribute**
Bobby	Helpful
Jim	Compassionate
Jerry	Professional/Gentleman
Barbara	Generous
Matt	Encourager

It is well known that self-discipline is a key factor in effective leadership. The habit of reading this list three times a day, every day, actually enhances your level of self-discipline. You not only will read this list, but you also will develop increased inner motivation to deal with other daily chores and routines.

Reading any list three times a day may seem quite excessive. However, did you realize that the average American looks at his or her watch over 80 times per day?

Now, that is excessive. If you think that is hard to believe, just try going without your watch for a day. If you don't wear a watch, then try moving the main clock in your house. You will soon find that you do look at your watch or clock many times during the day.

That being said, let's take a test. **Without** looking at your watch, answer these simple questions about it. Remember, no peeking!

- How does your watch mark the hours?
- Are there Roman numerals, Arabic numbers, dots, or slashes?
- Are they located at every hour or just the quarter hours?
- Are the markings at the 3, 6, 9, and 12 positions different from the rest?
- Is there a day and date indicator?
- What color is the face?
- Does your watch have more than one color on it?
- Is there any writing on the face?
- What color is the writing on the face?
- Does your watch have just two hands, or does it also have a second hand?

Ok, now look at your watch.

How did you do? If you are like 75% of the people who go through our seminars, you did not get even half the questions right. Now, once again, without looking at your watch, can you tell us what time it is?

"WHAT?" You mean to tell us that even after we asked you to look at your watch you cannot tell us what time it is? You look at your watch on an average of 80 times per day, but you cannot tell us what it looks like or even tell us what time it is. How much more important is studying your list of most admired attributes? Read the list three times per day, every day.

The magic, if you will, is not in the reading of the list or the habit of reading it. The true power comes in **why** you read the list. Read your list in the morning. Now, look for opportunities to practice something(s) on that list as the day progresses. At noon, read the list again. How many attributes have you practiced so far? Which ones do you still need to look for opportunities to accomplish? In the evening, read your list, looking to see which attributes you practiced and which ones you did not. Maybe this will give you a head start on which ones to look for first tomorrow.

If the list above were our list, we would start out our day looking for opportunities to be helpful, compassionate, professional, generous, and encouraging. We may not find opportunities for all of the attributes, but we should continue to look. The goal is to practice as many of the attributes as possible each day.

We are told that two of the recent U.S. Presidents at the turn of the century (one Democrat and one Republican) continue to practice this technique. One has used it for over 45 years and the other for more than 30 years. They both still read their list every day, three times a day.

We tell our clients that much of our work is inspired by John Maxwell's *"21 Irrefutable Laws of Leadership"* and Stephen Covey's *"7 Habits of Highly Effective People"*. We guarantee that if you read these works and practice them, you will become a stronger leader. However, we also guarantee that you will not be the best leader you can be unless you add these "21 Laws" and "7 Habits" in addition to your "6 Attributes." You see, the "21 Laws" are good, but they are not yours. The "7 Habits" are good, but they are not yours. The "6 Attributes" are core to you and who you are. These are the values, behaviors, or attitudes that have influenced you.

Read your list every day, three times a day.

My Personal Plan of Action

_____

_____

_____

_____

_____

_____

_____

_____

_____

_____

_____

 **Chapter 2**

How *Not* To Say, "No!"

*There is no limit to what can be done
if it doesn't matter who gets the credit.*

Author Unknown

Have you ever seen a child begging and pleading for the toy that he just could not live without? Have you been there when mom said, "no" and witnessed the fit that ensued? As adults, we are not that much different. None of us likes to be told "no." While leaders must have the ability to be decisive, they must always protect their interpersonal relationships with those whom they lead. For many employees, being told "no" damages the relationship. The dilemma for the leader arises when s/he has to tell a subordinate "no" but does not want the subordinates or their productivity to be adversely affected. How do you say "no" without saying "**no**"?

Our technique for not saying "no" consists of five steps:

1. Acknowledge the importance of the request/suggestion

2. State that you have a concern about the request/suggestion

3. Describe your concern

4. Offer an alternative or assistance

5. Keep that person involved

James has spent the majority of his career as a university professor and administrator. Something that seems to plague most universities is a preponderance of committees and committee work. Such was the case at one of his previous colleges at which he was on five committees! Faculty and staff members were grumbling at all the committee work they had to do. Often, it was difficult to do their main jobs because of the committee assignments. Yes, they complained. As a result, James eventually found himself chairing a sixth committee! He was to coordinate a committee to study committees.

James recalls:

> Soon afterward, I heard a colleague calling my name as I walked outside near one of our gardens. I spotted her bouncing toward me with great enthusiasm. As she drew near, she started telling me she had just heard that I was to chair the committee and that she had a great idea to solve the problem! I was glad to hear that, because I

did not have a clue what to do. Nancy began to explain her solution, "All we have to do is close the campus on Friday afternoons. No classes, no office hours, and no office operations. Then, schedule committee meetings on Friday afternoons." She was excited! What should I say to her? I could say, "Nancy, you have not thought this through, have you?" Maybe I would say, "No, no, no, that will not work. Just think about it." These kinds of responses do say, "no," but they also could jeopardize Nancy's productivity and our relationship. If I responded with such a reaction, what do you think would happen two weeks later if Nancy has another idea and it is a good one? She will not want to share it with me.

James effectively implemented the five-step technique:

Acknowledge the importance of the request:

"Nancy, I know what you mean. We have to find a way to get these assignments under control. It is affecting the entire campus."

State that you have a problem with the suggestion:

"Nancy, I think you are on the right track, but I have a concern about how it will work."

Describe your problem:

"Nancy, how many committees are you on?" She replies, "Four." "OK, on Friday afternoon all four committees are meeting; which one do you attend and which ones do you forsake?" "Oh," she says, "I did not think about that."

Offer an alternative or assistance:

"That's OK. I really think you may be on the right track. Do you know Mr. Yesbick?" She says, "Yes, I know Wayne." I say, "He is also concerned about this problem. Let me see if I can get the three of us working together."

Keep them involved:

"Would you mind visiting with Wayne about this? I am leaving town for a few days, and when I get back I will arrange for the three of us to get together and brainstorm. Nancy, I really like the way you think and know you can help with this."

With this technique, she leaves bouncing towards Wayne's office with the same energy with which she first approached James. The interpersonal relationship was not only protected but enhanced, and productivity was never adversely affected. Yet, he told her, "no." Real leaders never say "No."

My Personal Plan of Action

_____

_____

_____

_____

_____

_____

_____

_____

_____

_____

_____

_____

 # Chapter 3

Strengthening the Foundation

We all live under the same sky,
but we don't all have the same horizon.

Konrad Adenauer

A leader's compass is *Veritas* or "Truth Itself." True north is determined by what the leader honestly holds as most important in his or her life. Determining what is important and treating it as important is vital to the foundation of not only leadership but of the leader himself or herself.

This section examines and strengthens this foundation. You may be surprised what cornerstones are supporting your own foundation. Now let us examine and evaluate:

- **Your summa bonum**
- **Your inner circle**
- **5 "F's"**

Summa Bonum

It's not how much you make; it's how much you save.

Bobby McKinney

"Summa Bonum" is a Latin term meaning "greatest good". Don't know what yours is? Think about what the one thing people will remember about you when you die? For better or worse, that's your *summa bonum*. This is your legacy. So, what do you *want* it to be? Are you proud of yours, or do things need to change in your life? In short, the legacy you leave tomorrow is the one you live today. Strong leaders' leadership continues long after they are gone. It lives on because it is fueled by their legacy—their *summa bonum*. What's yours?

If I left today, I would be remembered as…

_____

_____

_____

I *want* to be remembered as…

_____

_____

_____

Inner Circle

Remember who has the butter.

Gail Hopkins

The "inner circle" is one of the strongest supports of our foundation and one of the most neglected. Notice the set of circles below. They form three rings similar to a target. The outer ring represents all your friends, yes, *all* of them, everyone you would consider to be a friend by any definition. Imagine their names written in that outer ring. You have to imagine it because you have too many to fit into the ring.

The second ring is more exclusive. Imagine that a loved one tells you that he is throwing a birthday party for you; however, he has rented a room that will hold only about 20-25 people. Whom would you like to invite? You go to your mental Rolodex of all your friends and pull down a list of your "good friends." For most of us, this is a group of 15-40 people. This is the second circle of friends. Within this second circle, there exists a small handful of friends who are very special. They are the ones whom you can tell anything. They will stick with you no matter what. These are your "best" friends. For most of us, we have 3-6 of these friends. These are in the inner circle of our friends.

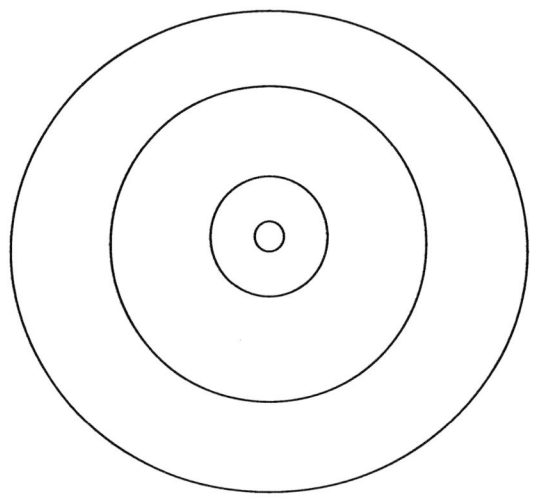

Inner Circle Exercise

1. Write down the names of your inner circle.

2. Evaluating each friend one by one, ask yourself this question. Is _____ helping me to grow into who I want to be and to go where I want to be? If the answer is "no", that friend cannot remain in your inner circle. Sometimes s/he can be moved to the second circle. Sometimes s/he has to be moved to the outer circle. Yes, this is tough! We are talking about removing your best friend. We all have had to do it, and James has had to do it twice. It is not easy.

3. Once you have validated your inner circle of friends, use them. Do whatever it takes to stay in their lives and keep them in yours no matter how many miles or years separate you.

One of our regular clients is a very well-known company that makes, among other things, delicious little chocolate candies that melt in your mouth and not in your hands. Frequently, we are asked to lead a seminar for their new junior executives on the importance of the inner circle. Why would a corporate giant be concerned about their executives' circle of friends? Well, here is a scenario that describes part of the concern.

These new executives have just "made it." They have just been given the salary which they have driven for, the corner office they have envied, and they have a parking spot with their name marking it; they have finally made it. Jim is one of these new executives. Jim comes home after work and discusses dinner plans with his wife, Jill. He begins, "Jill, let's call some friends and go out tonight." Jill answers, "Great, let's call John and Pam." Jim hesitates, "Jill, don't misunderstand me. John and Pam are our best friends and we will love them forever, but I thought we might eat at the country club tonight. The last time we took John and Pam they did not seem to feel comfortable at the club, because they are not members. And I know that John did not get the bonus he planned on using for a new car. I feel funny picking them up in our new Beemer. I mean, they will always be our friends, but maybe we need to find some new friends who can join in our new level of living. It will also be good for my career to make friends in a higher professional status than John and Pam…".

We hope Jim enjoys his new-found success. Research indicates that he will be there for less than 36 months before he falls! People do not realize that the people who got you on top are the same people who keep you on top. Both President George H. W. Bush and President Bill

Clinton had hand-picked advisors and hand-picked cabinets. Yet, when they had to make a decision of national security or one of a personal nature, they did not turn first to their advisors or the cabinets. They each have a list of five and six people, respectively, whom they called. The combined list includes both males and females. Of the 11 people on the combined list, only three are in the socio-economic level of the presidents. The list has people the men knew in teenage sports teams, college friends, neighbors whom they met while jogging. In other words, they are friends. And they still depend on them today.

Do not trade old friends for new.

Five "F's"

Never let the urgent replace the important.
Bill Hummel

This next exercise sometimes steps all over our toes. Begin by listing the five most important things in your life. If you have five children do not list them as your five points; just list them together as "family." Really, stop reading and take a moment to identify the five most important things in your life.

Without even knowing who you are, we can probably come really close to naming your items. And, we will do it by categorizing them under five "F's." We may not get them in order, but we will probably get most of them. Ready?

Family, Faith, Friends, Finance, and Fitness

How did we do? Even though most of us have a similar list, if not the same, many of us do not do well at all on the Urgency Test. We too often fall back on making the excuse that what we spend our time on is *for* the benefit of one of the five "F's" on our list. For example, we say that family is one of the most important things in our life. However, we spend about 60 hours a week working. We spend very little time with our families. Our typical excuse? We are working *for* my family. We also have found that there is a difference between spending time *with* God and spending time *for* God. Hummel's advice of never letting the urgent replace the important is a call to not just identify our priorities but to spend time with them.

James often tells the story of a young mother who had several children. One day, she left them outside while she ran a quick errand. When she returned, she found the children, along with some neighborhood children, huddled around something in her front yard. Getting out of her car, she approached the youngsters to see whatever it was that held their attention. She expected something like a pretty flower, a butterfly, or something similar. As she arrived, she found that the kids had gathered around a litter of baby skunks. Loudly, she yelled, "Quick, kids, run!" They each picked up a baby skunk and ran.

We all run, morning to night. Work non-stop. Hurry up and wait. Try to beat a deadline. Live in the fast lane. The sad part about our lifestyle is that we are good at it. But the price we pay is time with the most important people and things in our life.

My Personal Plan of Action

_____

_____

_____

_____

_____

_____

_____

_____

_____

_____

_____

_____

Chapter 4

Good - Great - Comfort - Confidence

Friendship is built upon the commitment to be a friend,
not upon the desire to have a friend.

Author Unknown

Jim Collins, in his best selling book, <u>Good to Great</u> identifies the characteristics of America's great companies. His research team conducted an exhaustive study and came up with some powerful observations. One of the characteristics inherent in great companies is leadership. Even though different company leaders had differing styles and approaches, they all had one thing in common: they had drive and humility. Most people understand about drive as a component of good leadership, but humility? If you think this is ironic, wait. It is not enough to be humble; a leader must demonstrate humility for subordinates to observe. In fact, some say that leaders do not have to be humble, as long as they appear humble to subordinates. A condition we frequently coach is when a leader is humble but subordinates never see the humility because of work load, environment, etc; therefore, they do not consider the leader to be humble. So, we need a technique that will allow subordinates to see drive and yet humility.

Exercise 1: Integrate Comfort and Confidence

The Ethos Leadership Group, Inc. has had great success coaching with the following technique. This technique develops behavioral habits that communicate drive and humility through two actions: meditation and practice.

Begin by spending time thinking about the two terms "comfort" and "confidence." We advise our clients to spend a couple of days deliberately ruminating over these words. We even ask them to write them on sticky notes and place them where they will be read throughout the day.

After two days of contemplation, spend two weeks of action. In every encounter practice comfort and confidence. In other words, do whatever it takes to make the other person feel comfortable while at the same time communicating strong self-confidence. Yes, every encounter, short or long, whether with one person or in a group. You must practice it whether you are holding a door open or negotiating a major contract.

In our respective jobs, we sometimes find ourselves facilitating committee meetings that last for hours. Still, we try to make each person feel as comfortable as possible (as appropriate), while always conveying confidence. To further integrate this practice, find small everyday opportunities to identify with and exhibit these traits. Consider opening doors for people; it takes only five seconds. Open the door in a way that will make the other person feel comfortable and concentrate on communicating confidence. You should look for these opportunities until it becomes second nature.

As you demonstrate comfort and confidence, you are perceived as having drive and humility. Try the exercise for two weeks. Record in writing at the end of each day what experiences you had. This will enhance the process of transforming your habit.

Exercise 2: ~~Say~~ *Write*, "Thank You."

A friend of ours and James' dear mentor in leadership, professionalism, and work ethic is Jerold Panas. Jerry is the principal partner of America's largest and oldest philanthropic consultancy. James credits Jerry for teaching him this exercise:

> He taught me to write, "Thank You." Today, I write more than 150 personal thank-you notes each month. Most of my notes go to donors. When I am in the office, I write them on university note cards. When I am traveling (which is about 50-60% of the time), the first thing I do when I step off the airplane is buy post cards representing the city I am visiting. I alter my typical message by beginning, "Dear_____, I am in Nashville today, but I want to thank you..." The response you will get is tremendous. People realize that you are writing while you are "away," this translates as drive. The fact that you went out of your way to say "Thank you" in a hand-written note is perceived as humility.

We are asked to teach this practice at the Institute for Charitable Giving. While teaching this in Washington D.C., people asked, "How do you discipline yourself to write so many notes?" They really were asking how they could stay motivated enough to write note after note after note every month. **The secret**: buy a pen that you think is beautiful and that you cannot afford. Also, *make sure* it feels good in your hand. If you get a true fountain pen, test the nib size and be certain you get the right point size for your handwriting. When you spend this amount of money, believe us, you will want to get it right. A couple pens we have found that work for us are a Mont Blanc special roller ball and a Pelikan M800 fountain pen. Even if we hate to write, we love to use these fine instruments. Each time we have given this advice, we have had people look at us with some serious doubt. Yet, after each time, we have had people contact us and tell us that the pens actually did make a significant difference in their note writing.

Write thank-you notes for everything, especially to your employees, members, and/or colleagues. Post cards to your members and employees go a long way in their view of your leadership. Let's face it; in an age of electronic communication, the value of a hand-written note is, and will continue to be, magnified. When is the last time you received a hand-written note or postcard? Did you not get at least a little excited to be getting "real mail?" This exercise also will magnify how others view your leadership.

My Personal Plan of Action

_____

_____

_____

_____

_____

_____

_____

_____

_____

_____

_____

_____

 **Chapter 5**

There You Are!

There are no hopeless situations;
there are only men who have grown
hopeless about them.

Motto of Marshall Ferdinand Foch,
the hero of Verdun

When we engage other people, our nonverbal actions communicate one of two messages: "Here **I** am" or "There **you** are!" The best leadership practice is to focus attention on others. Here are some secrets used by some of the most powerful leaders in America.

Secret 1: Their Name

When you meet someone for the first time, engage in a brief conversation. Do not leave the conversation until you have addressed them by his/her name at least three times. An example might go as follows:

Ted: James this is Bob McKinney. Bob, this is James Johnson.

James: Bob [1st time], it is a pleasure to meet you. I have heard good things about your work with the Chamber of Commerce.

Bob: Thanks, James. I have a lot of good people working with me.

James: Bob [2nd time] I heard you speak last month to the Rotary Club. I was truly impressed with your vision and plans for our region in economic development initiatives.

Bob: Thank you. I'm glad to hear that you were at the Rotary meeting. We would love to have you come back.

James: I will. Bob [3rd time], it really is a pleasure to meet you. I hope we have a chance to visit again very soon. I would enjoy getting together for lunch. Have a nice evening.

By calling Bob by name three times, you actually accomplish several things: you probably will not forget his name; you have affirmed him, therefore, establishing a degree of trust and credibility; plus, you may have just made a new friend.

Secret 2: Special Guest

This technique is especially useful if you are working with a sales client, donor, or someone whom you are going to make a request. The environment is lunch or dinner at a nice restaurant or club.

Let's say that you are having dinner with John and Pam Piersol at the club at 7:00. You should arrive no later than 6:30. Find out who your wait person will be and give him a very generous tip before your guests arrive. After all, the word "TIPS" came from an acronym, To Insurer Proper Service, and was originally given at the beginning of the meal. Also, give the wait person instructions for the evening. When the Piersols arrive, you are there to greet them. When you are all seated, your wait person approaches the table. His first words are, "Good evening, Ms. Piersol, welcome to the club. What would you like to drink this evening? He follows with, "Dr. Piersol, it is a pleasure to have you with us as well. May I bring you something to drink?"

Since John and Pam have never been to the club before, they know something special has happened for the waiter to know their names and address them first. You will score major relationship points with this technique. Another practice of "There **you** are!"

Often as leaders, one of the hardest things we have to do is to get over ourselves. To grow as a leader, the practice of "There **you** are!" is essential to grasp. As we travel the country conducting leadership seminars, we are often asked, if we could give only one piece of advice, what it would be. That's easily answered with, "It's *not* about *you*." There are never very many people who like hearing that. However, once we can convince someone that true leadership is about others and how we relate to them, then there will never be a shortage of people willing to follow. Remember, it's not, "Here **I** am"; it's "There **you** are!"

 **My Personal Plan of Action**

_____

_____

_____

_____

_____

_____

_____

_____

_____

_____

_____

_____

 **Chapter 6**

It Is Not About Unity

*The best way to promote unity
is to promote truth.*

Author Unknown

Many books on leadership spend a lot of ink on discussing the leader's responsibility in establishing, implementing, and preserving unity. Our clients have discovered that there is something advantageous in unity, but the real secret is in protecting *synergy*.

Textbooks often describe synergy as the whole being greater than the sum of its parts. We use the illustration of taking flour, eggs, sugar, milk, and baking powder and asking what would happen if you ate them all at once, jumped up and down, and stood out in the hot sun. Well, you're not going to get a cake; all you're going to get is "tossed cookies." Then, of course, they ask what would happen if you placed the same ingredients in a pan, stirred them together, and place them in an oven. The cake that would result would be a result of "unity" of the five individual ingredients combined in a process; that's evidence of **synergy**.

While many would teach would-be leaders to focus on unity, we coach clients to protect synergy. We ask the question, "When did the five ingredients become one cake?" When do five basketball players become one team? When do seven citizens become one council? When do four church leaders become one eldership? The answer is not possible to identify, because it does not just happen at a particular time. It is a process. And, like the cake, it usually happens after things have been stirred up and there has been a little heat. We define "synergy" as the process of unity. It is not unity; it is the process of unity. The most effective leaders protect the process, they protect synergy. What happens if one of the eggs that is going into the cake is bad? What happens if the mixture needs stirring? The best leaders focus on the process, not just the results.

My Personal Plan of Action

_____

_____

_____

_____

_____

_____

_____

_____

_____

_____

_____

 **Chapter 7**

More Brash Humility

Most people would rather get home
than get ahead.

Author Unknown

Three practices that would seem to be
commonplace tend to be severely neglected. They are
at the top of most executive coaches' "To Do List."
They are probably steps you have heard many times
before, but effective leaders work diligently to keep
them active in their daily behavior.

Practice 1: Apologize

Ken Blanchard puts the first practice as a one-word book title, "Apologize." Great leaders apologize. They apologize quickly, in few words, and face to face, if at all possible. They follow up with a very short hand-written note (25 words or fewer). The oral apology contains **responsibility** for the offense, **regret** for the consequences, and an offer to **repair** any damage. This is one of the most difficult things that a leader will ever do. It shows you are human, but also proves that you are a leader. The respect that you will gain from apologizing for a wrong will far out weigh the discomfort in taking that first step to apologize.

Responsibility Regret Repair

Practice 2: Sacrifice Rights

Leaders sacrifice personal rights and accept added responsibilities. Yes, most leaders put in at least a 50-hour work week. They do not get very many weekends off. Yet, when a great leader does get a Saturday off, do not be surprised to see her at a soccer game with one of her employees (or clients, donors, members, etc.), watching the employee's son play while his dad is fighting in the war. You may not see it, but great leaders come back to work late at night because they left at 3:00 p.m. to go visit with an employee who just learned that his wife wants a divorce. Great leaders are willing to sacrifice their rights.

Practice 3: Give Away Credit

When things go right, good leaders share the credit with the rest of the team. This is true (maybe more so) when the leader did happen to do most of the work. Consider the following scenario: The Board says, "Jeff, you really did a great job on that project. Wow! We are certainly proud of you." A great leader will reply with something like, "Thank you so much for the compliment, but I need you to know that it really was a team effort. I have never seen Scott work so hard on a project. And Carol gave up two weekends to come in so we would meet the target date. If it had not been for Kim covering for Brian when he got sick, I do not know what we would have done. The whole team did a super job." The Board knows that you were the catalyst. Now they also know that you are humble.

Why are these three practices so significant? Answer this question: "How do you determine if a leader is successful?" Is it the bottom line? Is it how many people he leads? Is it the size of the salary? Is it the items on the resume? Is it marked improvement in productivity and efficiency within the organization? No. The answer is:

The success of a leader is determined by the success of the people he leads.

When a leader realizes that her success depends on the success of her team, then attitudes, behaviors, and sometimes emotions change in a very positive direction.

My Personal Plan of Action

_____

_____

_____

_____

_____

_____

_____

_____

_____

_____

_____

# Chapter 8

Motivation and Affirmation

Inspiration without perspiration is a daydream;
perspiration without inspiration is a nightmare.

Author Unknown

There are several differences between a *boss* and a *leader*. One difference we focus on is an extension of dependence on the success of your subordinates, as mentioned in the previous section. It is imperative that, as a leader, you find ways to maintain relationships and find ways to motivate your employees. We have two techniques that have proven to be extremely beneficial in this regard.

Motivation Technique 1: A Gift

Have your employees complete a form that lists their favorites and important dates. Along with their hire date, birthday, anniversary, etc., capture things such as their favorite singer, band, pizza toppings, candy bar, fast food, restaurant, movie, actor, pastime, author, and anything else you think may be helpful. We have included an example for you in the back of the book (Appendix C).

After getting a form on each of your employees, design a spreadsheet or some type of tickler file that allows you to list each employee and the date that you give them one of their favorites. For example, Tim has been doing a great job lately, and I have not given him any special recognition. I look at his form and see that his favorite candy bar is a Payday. While he is away at lunch, I leave a Payday on his desk with a handwritten card thanking him for his hard work. I also know that Marty put in a lot of free overtime on our new DVD presentation. It seems like I just gave him some recognition not very long ago. I think it was movie tickets. I look at my tickler file and discover that I am right. I did give him movie tickets, but it was eight months ago! Wow, could it really have been that long ago? (That's why we use a tickler file…time does fly.) I buy the new CD by his favorite band and leave it for him with a handwritten note. While I was looking at the tickler file, I noticed that I have not given any recognition to our newest employee, and she has been with us for four months. She gets a handwritten note which reads, "Kim, you are really making a difference. I am so glad you are here!" with a gift card to the local bookstore (she likes to read).

Get the favorites list. Create a tickler file.
Check your tickler file regularly.

Motivation Technique 2: A Complementary Focus

Divide your team into groups of five or six. If your team is small in number, just have all members in one group. If not already sitting at round tables, have the groups sit in circles and instruct all members to take out a piece of paper and write their own name at the top. Next, have the members pass their papers to the left, so that all members hold the paper of the person seated to their right. As the members silently read the name at the top of the paper they receive, they quietly write something nice about that person on the paper. They may write something serious or humorous, but it must be complimentary. When everyone is finished, pass the paper to the left again. Members look to see whose paper they now have and write something complimentary. Continue to pass and write until the papers have gone all the way around the circle, **but stop** just prior to the papers returning to their owners. At this point, pass all the papers to a designated reader. Without revealing the names, the reader should read the compliments out loud, and the group should identify whom the compliments are given to. Do not attempt to identify the owner until the reader has read every compliment on the page. Give the owners their papers for them to keep. The readers must also read their own papers.

This exercise is fantastic as an icebreaker for a workshop, a prelude to teambuilding, or an opening for conflict resolution. It builds trust, affirmation, and communication flow.

My Personal Plan of Action

_____

_____

_____

_____

_____

_____

_____

_____

_____

_____

_____

_____

 **Chapter 9**

How a Leader Gives Criticism

Give each person you meet
the care and attention you would a friend,
and everyone you meet will be a friend.

Much like the section on "How to Say 'No'", this unit deals with some of the negative aspects of a leader's responsibilities. The technique offers 10 must-know steps for a positive outcome.

Giving Criticism Effectively

1. Confront only the one causing the harm.

   This is not only the ethical approach, but in most states it can be illegal to discuss details of one's performance to others. It creates what lawyers like to call "a hostile working environment."

2. Do not criticize in public.

   The rule of thumb is "Praise in Public, Criticize in Private." Also, violation of this rule could also cause a hostile working environment.

3. Do not compare an employee (or his or her behavior) to another's.

4. Make your complaint
   a. as soon as possible
   b. when in private
   c. when you have cooled down

5. Do not repeat a point once it has been understood.

6. Object only to actions the employee can modify.

7. Try to make only one complaint in the session.

8. After making the complaint, if it fits, do not apologize.

9. Do not overly preface the session. Get to the point quickly!

10. Avoid sarcasm. Keep *everything* professional.

Important considerations:

Do not have your office as the default place for criticism interviews. Many times it is more effective to have it in the employee's office or even while taking a walk.

If there is a chance that the problem may lead to termination or has involved illegal activity, you must have someone else in the session as a witness. Instruct the witness (it is good to have someone whom the employee trusts) that he must remain quiet. His job is simply to be there. If the employee asks him something, he may answer the question but should not engage in conversation.

Do not expect employees to respond well to criticism if you have never complimented them.

Termination: If you are terminating an employee, try this method. Have a witness in the room. Have a very professional packet compiled that includes severance information, insurance information, letter of recommendation (if appropriate), a letter of dismissal and any other information you deem expedient. Place this in a very nice folder. When the employee comes in, have him take a seat and begin with something like,

> John, thanks for coming in. I am sorry to inform you that the company is making some cuts and your position is being

eliminated. I have a folder of information for you that should answer most of your questions. Please take it and read it. If you have questions or just want to talk, call me the day after tomorrow and we will get together. I think you should leave the building right now and read the folder. Come back around 7:00 tonight and we will help you clean out your desk. John, again feel free to call me Thursday.

You want to avoid out-of-control emotions. Give him the folder. Let him know that today is not the day for conversation. You can talk in two-three days. Do not let the employee get a word-game or blame-game started. If he tries, stop him by telling him that he can call you the day after tomorrow. This can certainly be an uncomfortable situation, but you must maintain control. Stay calm, focused, and insistent that the time to talk is in a few days. This is essential.

If possible, try to dismiss employees late in the afternoon and early in the week. Avoid the 4:45 p.m. Friday meeting.

My Personal Plan of Action

_____

_____

_____

_____

_____

_____

_____

_____

_____

_____

_____

_____

# Summary

The summary is up to you; it literally is in your hands. Below is a one-month executive coaching plan utilizing these exercises to help you muscle-up your leadership. Realize that most of the practices prescribed below do not begin and end in a single week. For example, in week one you will create your list of qualities and start using them. You will continue to use them from now on, not just in week 1. If you desire additional assistance or would like to give us an update on your progress, feel free to contact us.

We would love to hear how these exercises are changing your leadership and attracting followers you never dreamed.

Contact us at:

Ethos_james@hotmail.com   Dr. James Johnson

Ethos_matt@hotmail.com   Matt Rush

Ethos_angela@hotmail.com   Angela Johnson

Or by phone: 1-800-299-3460

Your One-Month Executive Coaching Plan

Session	Activity	Personal Observations/Experiences
Week 1	Create your list of "Attributes" and begin reading them three times a day, looking for opportunities to practice them.	
Week 1	Read The 21 Irrefutable Laws of Leadership by John Maxwell. Take Notes.	
Week 2	Spend the entire week looking for opportunities to practice the "Comfort and Confidence" exercise. Take notes.	
Week 2	Evaluate your inner-circle. Reconnect with friends, remove negative influences.	
Week 3	Begin each day this week by telling yourself, "My purpose today is to make three people smile." Do it.	
Week 3	Read Who Moved My Cheese by Spencer Johnson. Take notes.	
Week 4	Buy an expensive pen such as a Mont Blanc, Pelikan, or similar. Purchase some high quality stationary cards. For pens: www.coloradopen.com. For stationary (correspondence cards) check: www.americanstationary.com item #HBC	
Week 4	Look for at least 6 opportunities to practice "There You Are!" Make notes on the effects.	

Appendix A

Leaders on Leadership

Joshua

There are too many leaders to list as examples or resources of good leadership. However, there are three leaders which you could do well to study. The first one is found in the Old Testament. His leadership lesson can be read on one page. On the first page of the book of Joshua, God tells a reluctant leader to "Be Strong and Be Courageous". In fact, God tells him three times! The second time, God also tells Joshua to "remember my word." If only one leadership lesson could be taught, this would be it. Think what would have been if WorldCom, Tyco, and Oral Roberts University leaders would have just followed the three parameters of leadership in Joshua 1.

Be Strong!

Be Courageous!

Behave!

Ken Blanchard

Ken Blanchard is one of our favorite authors. In 2002 he invited James Johnson to write a chapter in a book *Conversations on Success*, with Dianna Booher and Ty Boyd. Of the more than 25 books written by Ken Blanchard, probably the most unique is his 2003 *The One Minute Apology*. The one point he makes for strong leadership is the humility and skill to apologize. His keys to apologizing include:

- Realize and admit you are wrong

- Deal personally with any damage you have caused

- The longer you wait to apologize, the sooner your weakness is perceived as wickedness

- Never get upset with yourself, just your behavior

Winston Churchill

Most, if not all, college courses on leadership give significant time and attention to the attributes and behaviors of Winston Churchill. His wit, determination, passion, and Cuban Punch cigar have contributed to his indelible watermark on the pages of many leadership pages.

Reviewing Churchill's leadership qualities, four aspects appear to be rudimental. These four features set him apart from other politicians and above mediocrity. Read the four aspects. Study how Churchill demonstrated them. Consider how you can practice them.

1. Candor and Plain Speaking

Maxim:

I have often had to eat my words, and I must confess that I have always found it a wholesome diet.

2. Decisiveness

Churchill liked to deliberate and make firm decisions.

Maxims:

Ponder and then act.

An accepted leader has only to be sure of what it is best to do or at least to have made up his mind about it.

3. Balanced attention to details with a view of the wider scene

Maxim:

An efficient and successful administration manifests itself equally in small as in great matters.

4. Held a historical imagination that informed his judgment

<u>Maxim</u>:

The longer you look back, the farther you can look forward.

Appendix B

Crab Cakes and Coaches

How to Select the Best Executive Coaching Firm

My career had *finally* started coming together. It sure seemed to take a lot longer than it should have, but things were good. I still knew that I could go up at least one more level. I just did not know how to get there. I had watched a friend named Karen struggle with her career during the same time I was building mine. However, after a few years at a level I judged to be behind my own, she passed me. Something changed in her. She appeared more confident. Her communication style became more effective. A new buzz hummed through the building about her powerful negotiation skills—skills I never knew she had. Her client list went from very good to a regional *Who's Who* list. My curiosity (maybe jealousy) got the best of me. I *had* to try and find out what she was doing!

Choosing an Executive Coaching Firm

Find a firm that assigns you more than just one coach.

Most good firms will design a plan that uses 4 to 8 different coaches for each client. Be careful of individuals who claim to be experts in many areas.

Use a firm that conducts pre-assessment and pre-coaching assignments.

This is usually a tip-off if the plan they create for you is unique versus if they simply have one plan they use for everyone.

Try to avoid hometown firms.

This is not set in stone, but you need to consider some degree of anonymity in your own location.

Do not be surprised if the firm does not have individual references.

Most of the best firms work in total confidence with their clients and protect that confidentiality.

It was a little awkward waiting for her to show up. After all, I had called her and asked if she would meet me for lunch. When she asked the purpose of the visit, I told her I had noticed some remarkable changes in her professional demeanor. She laughed and told me that *she would host me* for lunch and to meet at her club.

I arrived just a few minutes early. I had never been to this club and I was not too sure how things worked, so I waited in the lobby downstairs for her to arrive. She arrived right on time and we went up to the club where we were quickly and courteously greeted by the host. He greeted me by name! How did he know my name? Anyway, he escorted us to our table and a waiter approached, also greeting me by name, welcoming me to the club and asking what I would prefer to drink. "Karen," I asked, "Did you tell them my name?" "Yes," she replied, "I always call ahead and give them the last name of my guests and request that they be greeted. You would be surprised how many new clients I have gained by using this type of technique." I almost fell out of my chair when she told me that she learned this from her "executive coaches." I had never met *anyone* in my circles who had used a business or executive coach before! I was really taken aback by the thought that Karen would hire a coach. What could she possibly gain? She already had a B.S. in Business from a prestigious university and held an M.B.A. from one of the top schools in the nation!

The next forty-five minutes went by in a flash as we dined on spinach salad, crab cakes, Jamaican coffee, and the creamiest caramel-covered bread pudding anyone could imagine. As we enjoyed lunch, Karen explained what all she had learned from her coaches. I listened with some skepticism at first. I mean, what could an executive coach possibly teach me that I had not already learned in college or read from my trips to *Barnes & Noble*? That is when Karen corrected me. She said, "My coaches *do* teach me things, but more significantly, they *coach me* to win." She said, "They work like your old college baseball coaches. They've taken the skills and knowledge I already had and helped me to develop and apply them. And yes, they also taught me a lot of things I never knew before."

Her coaches did not have a "cookie-cutter" approach. Rather, they formulated a personal, calculated coaching plan for her unique qualities, aiming toward her desired goals. I was astonished by her description of her "pre-assessment" and "pre-coaching" appointments. These were sessions and assignments that she had to do before the coaches would even talk about a coaching plan. And then, just about the time we were served the bread pudding, came the main course of the conversation. Karen told me about her personal coaching plan.

Her plan consisted of eight different coaches each spending at least half a day with her once a month, teaching, coaching, challenging and giving her homework. She learned some of the most powerful negotiation skills I have ever seen. She even learned how to modify them depending on her client's own personality. She fascinated me by sharing some of the communication strategies she developed like how to say "no" in a positive way and how to deliver criticism effectively. She gently laughed as she told me that one of her favorite sessions was learning how to keep from being manipulated by a committee or group and also how she could maneuver a small group in a positive way. Later, I got to observe one of her departmental staff presentations. I was amazed at the delivery skills and the little things I noticed that came from her coaching. Her presentation was by far the most effective and enjoyable one of the day. Furthermore, she learned not only how to identify others' business personality types in just moments, but also how to modify her persuasion, negotiation and communication practices to be the most effective in light of their personalities. Her coaches even designed custom-tailored clothes that fit her to the tee—not just in cut, but to fit her personality, environment, and her own professional image. And I can tell you that she never looked or felt more confident!

After our lunch I started searching and investigating executive coaching firms for myself. Today, five years after the crab cakes, I have seen my own professionalism and leadership literally explode. My client list is what I only dreamed it would be. But more satisfying than my client list is the way I feel about myself and my professional confidence. Thanks, Karen. I still owe you lunch.

(After his own positive coaching experience, Dr. Johnson joined with some of the nation's top coaches and established the prestigious Ethos Leadership Group, Inc. based in Washington, D.C. Ethos has supplied coaches and leadership training America's top corporate and political leaders.)

Appendix C

Employee Data

Name:	
Birthday:	
Hire Date:	
Wedding Anniversary:	
Spouse's Name:	
Spouse's Birthday:	
Children's Names:	
Children's Birthdays:	

EMPLOYEE FAVORITES

Office Use Only	Favorites	Print Your Favorites
	Music genre:	
	Singer/band:	
	Candy bar:	
	Beverage:	
	Type of food:	
	Pizza topping:	
	Fast-food restaurant:	
	Chain restaurant:	
	Upscale restaurant:	
	Movie genre:	
	Actor:	
	Book genre:	
	Author:	
	Spare time activities:	
	Hobbies:	
	Desired gift(s) under $20:	
	Desired gift(s) under $10:	

Bibliography

Blanchard, Ken; Johnson, James; Booer, Dianna; Boyd, Ty. *Conversations on Success*. Insight Publishing, Severville, TN 2004.

Blanchard, Ken and McBride, Margret. *The One Minute Apology*. William Morrow Publishing, NY 2003.

Hayward, Steven. *Churchill on Leadership*. Gramercy Books, NY 2004.

Holton, Bill. *Leadership Lessons Of Robert E. Lee*. Gramercy Books, NY 1995

Johnson, James. *Communication for Effective Christian Service*. Academic Christian, Lubbbock, Texas 1989

Johnson, James. *The Difference between a Boss and a Leader*. Ethos Publishing, Vienna 2006

Lencioni, Patrick. *The Five Temptations of A CEO*. Jossey-Bass, NY 1965

Maxwell, John. *The 21 Irrefutable Laws of Leadership*. Thomas Nelson Publishers, Nashville 1998

 **About The Authors**

Dr. James A. Johnson

Dr. James A. Johnson has been noted as an expert in leadership for many years. His career includes teaching leadership and communication as a university professor (tenured at two institutions), serving as a university administrator from being a department chair to a president. In 1988, he established a leadership consultancy which boasts a who's who list of corporate and political clients. The list includes former U.S. Presidents, Senators, and Governors. Corporate clients include M&M Mars, Pedigree, Uncle Ben's Rice, Georgia Pacific, Cooper Tire and Rubber, Wells Fargo, and Bank of America. Dr. Johnson has been formally recognized by the Texas House and Senate, The State of Georgia, and the Governor of West Virginia. He has received the L.E.R.N. 2002 Award and was named "Scholar of Communication" in 1993 by the Western Social Science Association. James is also in constant demand as a major fundraiser and fundraising strategist having raised more than $50 million for various campaigns and projects.

Matthew D. Rush

Matthew D. Rush, President of the Ethos Leadership Group, is known throughout the country for his speaking ability, sales experience, and exuberant personality. His client base includes major corporations like M&M Mars, Los Alamos National Labs, National Safety Association, American Council on Germany, Texas Tech University, along with numerous not-for-profits.

He has been an invited guest of the White House and has been honored on the floor of the New Mexico House of Representatives. He has extensive experience in fund raising and holds a certificate of completion from the University of Indiana School of Philanthropy. In 2003, he was selected as the Students in Free Enterprise Alumnus of the Year. He currently serves on the Washington, D.C. based, Foundation for Agriculture Board of Directors, the Berean Children's Home Board of Directors, as well as a member ex-officio of the Students in Free Enterprise Board of Directors, past chairman of the Alumni Relations Taskforce. In his free time, he keeps himself busy on his farm and ranch in Eastern New Mexico.

Angela N. Johnson

Angela N. Johnson currently teaches in the West Virginia University system. Angela has taught communication courses in the U.S. as well as teaching full-time in China at Wuhan Polytechnic University. She also studied art in Italy. Angela received a B.A. in Organizational Communication with a 4.00 GPA graduating from her university as the top over-all graduate. She received a M.A. from West Virginia University through the prestigious, yet demanding, accelerated residence program. Ms. Johnson has worked as an Executive Coach with a major national firm since 2003. Angela is an expert in gender communication within leadership roles and organizational leadership.